P9-DXD-543

GLOBAL CULTURES

Mexican Culture

Lori McManus

Heinemann
LIBRARY
Chicago, Illinois

www.capstonepub.com
Visit our website to find out
more information about
Heinemann-Raintree books.

To order:
☎ Phone 800-747-4992
💻 Visit www.capstonepub.com
to browse our catalog and order online.

Edited by Charlotte Guillain, Abby Colich,
and Vaarunika Dharmapala
Designed by Steve Mead
Original illustrations © Capstone Global
Library Ltd 2013
Illustrations by Oxford Designers & Illustrators
Picture research by Ruth Blair
Originated by Capstone Global Library Ltd
Printed and bound in China by Leo Paper
Products Ltd

16 15 14 13 12
10 9 8 7 6 5 4 3 2 1

Library of Congress Cataloging-in-Publication
Data
McManus, Lori.
  Mexican culture / Lori McManus.
    p. cm.—(Global cultures)
  Includes bibliographical references and index.
  ISBN 978-1-4329-6783-3 (hb)—ISBN 978-
1-4329-6792-5 (pb) 1. Ethnology—Mexico—
Juvenile literature. 2. Mexico—Social life and
customs—Juvenile literature. I. Title.
  GN560.M6M39 2012
  305.800972—dc23   2011037707

Acknowledgements
We would like to thank the following for
permission to reproduce photographs: Alamy
pp. 6 (© Diana Bier Coyotepec), 7 (© Blake
Shaw), 8, 37 (© Danita Delimont), 12 (©
David Ball), 18 (© World Pictures), 20 (©
Jim West), 21 (© Keith Dannemiller), 22 (©
Marcin Mikolajczuk), 31 (© Charles O. Cecil),
32 (© Frans Lemmens), 35 (© Richard Ellis);
Corbis pp. 5 (© Ann Johansson), 9, 29 (©
Keith Dannemiller), 11 (© Susana Gonzalez/
DPA), 14 (© Jeremy Woodhouse/Blend
Images), 15 (© Jorge Rios Ponce/DPA), 16 (©
M.L. Sinibaldi), 17 (© Stuart Westmorland),
23 (© Tyrone Turner/National Geographic
Society), 24 (© Macduff Everton), 25 (©
Lindsay Hebberd), 26 (© Ocean), 30 (©
Richard Franck Smith/Sygma), 38 (© Danny
Lehman), 39 (© Patrick Lane/Somos Images),
40 (© Mario Guzman/EPA), 41 (© Dannie
Walls); Getty Images p. 13 (Hulton Archive);
Shutterstock pp. 27 (© Frontpage), 28 (© Bill
Perry), 43 top left (© B. Speckart), 43 top right
(© Bill Perry), 43 bottom left (© PSHAW-
PHOTO), 43 bottom left (© Paul Prescott),
design features (© wikkie).

Cover photograph of a smiling Mexican
girl reproduced with permission of Corbis
(© Bertrand Gardel/Hemis). Cover design
feature of a colourful textile reproduced with
permission of Shutterstock (© wikkie).

Every effort has been made to contact
copyright holders of any material reproduced
in this book. Any omissions will be rectified in
subsequent printings if notice is given to
the publisher.

All the Internet addresses (URLs) given in this
book were valid at the time of going to press.
However, due to the dynamic nature of the
Internet, some addresses may have changed, or
sites may have changed or ceased to exist since
publication. While the author and publisher
regret any inconvenience this may cause
readers, no responsibility for any such changes
can be accepted by either the author or the
publisher.

CONTENTS

Some words are shown in bold, **like this**. You can find out what they mean by looking in the glossary.

INTRODUCING MEXICAN CULTURE

It is a *fiesta* day in Mexico! Colorful paper decorations hang in the town **plaza**. Friends, neighbors, and families gather to eat, drink, and dance. Fire crackers light up the early morning or evening sky.

What is culture?

Culture is the values, beliefs, and attitudes of a particular place. It is about how people live and worship, and about the music, art, and literature they produce. *Fiestas* are just one part of Mexico's lively, colorful culture. Mexican culture combines **customs**, music, art, and beliefs from ancient **civilizations**, Europeans who have moved to Mexico, and the modern world.

Did you know?

The word "Mexico" comes from the group of native people who lived in central Mexico between 1325 and 1500 CE. These people were called *Mexica* (say "me-shee-ka"). Today, they are best known as the Aztecs.

The Olmecs developed the first civilization in the region of Mexico around 1500 BCE. Over the next 2,000 years, other **native** peoples built complex civilizations. Spain took control of Mexico from 1519 until 1821 CE and spread the **Roman Catholic** religion there. Today, about 80 percent of Mexicans are Roman Catholic. However, many Mexicans also follow native customs. This combination of beliefs and customs creates a unique Mexican culture today.

On December 12, Mexican people gather to eat, dance, and celebrate Our Lady of Guadalupe. This Catholic festival honors Mary, the mother of Jesus.

THE ART AND COLOR OF MEXICO

People in Mexico have been creating art for thousands of years. Starting around 1500 BCE, native artists made sculptures of ancient gods, and created pottery, jewelry, and **embroidery**.

Mexican folk art

Mexico has a long **tradition** of folk art – art that is handmade by native, working people for practical purposes. Since 900 BCE, **weaving** has been used to create blankets, rugs, clothing, and baskets.

Today, colorful patterns appear on items woven from wool, cotton, silk, bark, and grasses. Other craftspeople make long-lasting hats, purses, belts, and saddles out of leather.

This woman and her family create handmade black pottery in Oaxaca, Mexico. Pottery remains a popular art form because of its decorative appearance and practical use in cooking.

During the last 100 years, factories in Mexican cities have produced rugs, baskets, and pottery by machine. Even though craft-making has become a big business in cities, families in **rural** areas still create unique, handmade pieces. The adults pass their skills on to their children so that the folk art tradition continues.

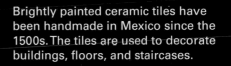

Brightly painted ceramic tiles have been handmade in Mexico since the 1500s. The tiles are used to decorate buildings, floors, and staircases.

7

Traditional clothing and costumes

In rural areas, Mexicans often dress in clothing made in traditional ways. Women wear loose pueblo dresses or skirts and short-sleeved blouses embroidered with colorful designs. Men wear simple pants, white cotton shirts, and leather sandals called *huaraches*. In these areas, men often wear large woven blanket capes called *serapes*. Some **indigenous** Mexican women wear skirts with long **tunics** called *huipiles*. The style of traditional clothing varies by region.

These Tzotzil Mayan women are wearing traditional clothing.

In Mexico, special costumes are worn only during holiday celebrations. Women wear long, colorful dresses with low-heeled shoes. These dresses have wide skirts that flow into the air when the women dance. Men dress in dark pants with bright trim on the sides. They also wear short suit jackets and boots.

Clothing in cities

In cities, Mexicans wear modern clothing similar to Americans and Europeans. Business people wear suits. Doctors, nurses, and police wear uniforms. Factory workers wear comfortable pants or skirts and shirts. Away from the coast, Mexican women dress modestly. They rarely wear sleeveless tops or shorts. People in smaller towns wear modern clothing, but might add cowboy hats or *huaraches*.

College students in Mexico dress casually in modern clothes such as T-shirts and tennis shoes.

YOUNG PEOPLE

Mexican children often wear comfortable clothing such as jeans and T-shirts when they are at home. Most children wear uniforms to school. A boy's uniform typically includes pants and a polo shirt. Girls usually wear skirts and blouses.

Paper arts

In Mexico, paper has been used for ceremonies and decorations since ancient times. The Otomi Indians still prepare paper from tree bark by hand. The bark paper is used to make paper dolls that represent humans, animals, and spirits. Mexican artists from the state of Guerrero paint colorful animals, village scenes, and flowers on bark paper. The tradition of bark painting dates back to 1200 BCE.

Mexicans artists use paper mache to create dolls, *piñatas*, and wall decorations. Pieces of paper are torn into strips and soaked in glue. The strips are then layered onto a frame to form a certain shape. Once dry, the shape is painted with bright colors or decorated with tissue and foil.

Papercuts (*papel picado*) are a popular decoration during holidays and festivals. Bright tissue paper is folded and cut with scissors to create different patterns. The papers are then glued together to form colorful banners. Skilled craftspeople use special tools to cut more complicated designs in tissue paper, such as skeletons and animals.

Did you know?

Tattoos have been part of traditional Mexican culture for thousands of years. Even today, Mexicans choose tattoos with religious designs from the native Maya and Aztecs. Another popular design is Our Lady of Guadalupe, an important figure in the Roman Catholic religion. Mexican flag tattoos show pride in Mexican culture and identity.

Masks

For thousand of years, Mexicans have created masks for use in religious ceremonies and festivals. Most folk art masks show animal faces with human emotions. Other masks look like characters from religious stories, including devils, angels, and kings. Most traditional Mexican masks are carved from wood and then painted. Other masks are made from paper mache, leather, clay, or metal.

These skeleton masks are worn during the Day of the Dead (see pages 25 and 30).

Murals have a message

The tradition of painting **murals** dates back to the Maya Indians (200 BCE–CE 900). Long ago, colorful murals showed scenes of rich people enjoying life. In modern times, murals often show important scenes from Mexican history or the problems faced by common working people. Some artists use murals to share their beliefs about how the government should treat people.

The most famous Mexican muralists of the 1900s were Diego Rivera, José Clemente Orozco, and David Alfaro Siqueiros. These artists are known as "The Big Three." The Big Three have influenced more recent Mexican artists to paint about real life experiences.

In Mexico, murals, such as this one by Diego Rivera, are often used to decorate public spaces and buildings.

Present-day art

Artists in present-day Mexico often show historical subjects or feelings about modern life in ways that are unusual, funny, and sometimes scary. For example, Carlos Amorales expresses fears in his video productions by constantly changing the shapes of dangerous creatures. Present-day artists often use non-traditional materials such as computer graphics, video, words combined with pictures, and photographs.

Frida Kahlo (1907–1954)

As a teenager, Frida Kahlo was seriously injured in a traffic accident. While she was recovering, Kahlo began to paint self-portraits that expressed her pain. She painted over 50 self-portraits during her lifetime. Kahlo always made her eyebrows look like they touched each other. She also painted flowers, fruits, and images of indigenous Mexican **heritage**. Kahlo's unique, simple style of painting made her famous.

MUSIC AND MOVEMENT

Lively music fills the air at Mexican gatherings and celebrations. Dancing is just as common. Some dances are familiar throughout Mexico, while other dances are unique to particular regions.

Mariachi bands are groups of male musicians who play traditional songs as they walk through plazas and restaurants.

Juan Gabriel (born 1950)

Born as Alberto Aguilera Valadez, this famous Mexican singer and songwriter took the stage name Juan Gabriel in his late teens. Gabriel combines different styles in his music, including mariachi and *ranchera*. He has won many international music awards.

Music fills the air

Mexicans listen to many types of music, from classical to rock. In village plazas, musicians often play Mexican folk songs on guitars, violins, and *marimbas* (a type of xylophone). Some folk songs have existed for hundreds of years, like the popular song "La Cucaracha" (which means "the cockroach").

Traditional Mexican music is played by mariachis and *bandas*. Mariachi bands usually consist of one singer, several men playing violins and trumpets, and a guitar player. Mexicans often dance to mariachi music because of its strong rhythms.

Bandas consist of 10 to 20 musicians playing mostly brass instruments, such as trumpets, trombones, and tubas. They usually have one lead singer with several back-up singers. *Bandas* are most famous for playing *ranchera* music from the rural areas of Mexico. *Ranchera* songs communicate feelings about nature, love, and patriotism. *Ranchera* music can have a slow or fast beat.

Dancing through life

Mexican people dance on important occasions to express feelings and religious beliefs. Dance keeps Mexicans in touch with their native heritage. Mexicans seem to have a dance for every kind of event: births, deaths, weddings, rainstorms, harvests, and even old age.

These dancers are wearing traditional festival costumes.

The Mexican Hat Dance is the national dance of Mexico. This dance tells the story of new love and is performed by one couple or a group of couples. The performers dance with quick hopping steps around a wide-brimmed hat called a sombrero.

The Dance of the Deer has been performed in Mexico for centuries. The dance illustrates a deer hunt, with performers playing the roles of the deer and the hunters. Instruments such as rattles and flutes create a dramatic mood for the dance. Other traditional dances also copy the movements of native animals, such as the iguana (a type of lizard).

In the Dance of the Deer, performers with headdresses portray deer while the hunters wear wooden masks.

Ballet folklórico

Mexican ballet folklórico groups perform dances with pointed toes and large, graceful movements. Started in 1952, ballet folklórico combines modern dance techniques with traditional Mexican costumes and music. The dances tell stories of ancient gods and rulers. The colors used for ballet folklórico costumes depend on the region from which the dancers come.

Ballet folklórico is a colorful and vibrant dance form.

YOUNG PEOPLE

Mexican children often learn traditional dances such as the Mexican Hat Dance at school. Some children and young adults join ballet folklórico groups. These groups practice for long hours so they can perform with excellence in front of audiences. Participating in ballet folklórico trains the students in important traditions and modern dances.

Unique regional dances

Mexico is divided into 31 states. Each state has particular dances that show that state's history.

Dancers perform the Mexican Agricultural Dance in the state of Guerrero. This dance comes from Aztec beliefs about clearing the land to grow crops such as corn. Dancers crack whips to imitate the sounds of burning bushes. Other dancers copy the movements of animals that run away as the fire burns.

In Yucatan, dancers raise their hands and copy the sound of castanets with their fingers. Castanets are wooden instruments clapped together with fingers. They were brought to Yucatan by Spanish **colonists** in the 1500s.

Settlers from Germany, Poland, and Austria brought dances such as polkas and waltzes to the Mexican states of Nuevo León and Chihuahua. These European rhythms were combined with indigenous Mexican movements to create fast-paced dances in these regions.

FAMILY AND RELATIONSHIPS

Mexicans value family relationships, loyalty, and traditions. They share clear ideas about proper behavior at home and in public. As they grow up, Mexican children learn respectful ways of relating to other people.

The traditional family

Traditionally, Mexican families are large, with a father, mother, and three or more children. In cities, parents tend to have just one or two children. Many Mexican families have close, caring relationships.

Traditional Mexican mothers spend hours in the kitchen each day preparing fresh meals for their families.

Fathers in traditional families work to provide clothing, shelter, and food for their wives and children. They make decisions and protect the family. Traditionally, women take care of the home, cook meals, and raise the children. Mothers are admired for their devotion to the family, but the father is the head of the home.

Modern families

The roles of family members have changed in recent years. In modern cities, many women now choose to attend college and take jobs as doctors, lawyers, and business owners. When children are born, the women often continue to work and run the family home. Most Mexican husbands have not yet started to share housekeeping chores.

Did you know?

In Mexico, children are usually given two last names at birth. The first name is the father's last name; the second name is the mother's last name.

Mexican families in rural areas tend to be large. This father and mother live together with their seven children.

Mexican children

Most Mexican children tend to be happy and well-behaved. Parents teach their children to be polite, to respect adults, and to work together for the good of the family. Mexican children often live in their parents' home until their mid-20s, especially if they come from a wealthy family.

YOUNG PEOPLE

Mexican children love to play games and sports. Jump rope and baseball are popular. Some Mexican children also like *jai alai*, a sport played inside a closed court using basket paddles and a ball. Children often play *Lotería*, a game similar to bingo using picture cards and songs.

Soccer is the most popular sport in Mexico. Children often play soccer on the streets in their local neighborhoods.

In Mexico, all children are supposed to attend primary school for six years. Most children in cities and large towns complete these early years of education. However, some families cannot afford to buy the books or supplies their children need. Instead, the children work to help feed the family. Some rural families do not live close to a school.

Did you know?

Spanish is the official language of Mexico. Yet almost 100 native languages are spoken around the country. More than 80 percent of people who speak a native language also speak Spanish. Some families who only speak an indigenous language do not send their children to school, since lessons are taught in Spanish.

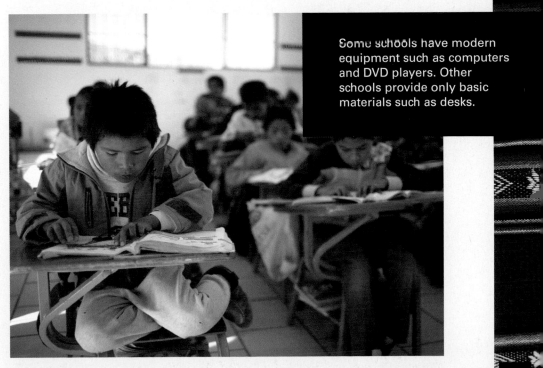

Some schools have modern equipment such as computers and DVD players. Other schools provide only basic materials such as desks.

The extended family

In Mexico, several **generations** of extended family often live together in the same house. The extended family includes grandparents, aunts, uncles, and cousins. Many families choose to live together because these relationships are just as important as those in the **nuclear family**. Often, families live together because they are poor and cannot afford separate homes.

Even when extended families do not live together, they gather frequently for celebrations and to share meals. While eating together, family members can share stories and problems. Many Mexicans feel a duty to help family members with money, health, or work problems.

Can you guess the relationships of these members of an extended family?

In Mexico, the extended family also includes godparents. These individuals are chosen by a baby's parents at the time of his or her **baptism**. Traditionally, godparents were responsible for making sure the child received training in the Roman Catholic religion. In modern times, godparents are often expected to take an active interest in the child's development as a person. In return, many godparents receive affection, loyalty, and respect from their godchildren.

Each *ofrenda* has photographs and items that the family member enjoyed in life.

Did you know?

Mexicans show respect and care for their extended family members even after death. During a yearly holiday called Day of the Dead, families set up **altars**, or *ofrendas* (see page 30), in their homes to honor relatives who have died. Favorite foods, drinks, and personal items are placed on the altars as gifts to the spirits of the dead relatives.

Relationships outside the family

In Mexico, most relationships start off formally. When first introduced, Mexicans use the respectful titles of *Don* and *Doña* before a person's last name. Mexicans do not use a person's first name until invited to do so. The word "you" has formal and informal forms in Spanish. Children always use the formal term with adults. Adults use the formal term with other adults until they know them well.

Mexicans often greet each other with a formal handshake or grasp on the arms. Close friends and relatives hug and kiss each other.

Typically, Mexicans use polite, gentle words to enter a conversation. If a serious business agreement needs to be discussed, the individuals will talk about friendly subjects first. In Mexico, people try to avoid conflict in conversations.

Did you know?

Mexico City, the capital of Mexico, is home to almost 20 million people! The streets and highways are usually crowded with cars and buses. While normally polite in conversation, some Mexicans become angry and rude when stuck in heavy traffic.

Mexicans pay close attention to rank in business and society. They give authority and respect to people with higher status than themselves. For example, Mexicans who work on farms or in factories look to professionals such as teachers, lawyers, or business owners to make decisions for their cities and villages.

Mexico City contains tall office buildings, modern shops, sports stadiums, parks, restaurants, apartments, and houses. Millions of people live close together in and around the city.

MEXICAN CELEBRATIONS

In Mexico, *fiestas* occur frequently throughout the year. Mexicans gather on these holidays to eat, dance, take part in parades, watch fireworks, and remember historic or religious events. However, celebrations are not limited to holidays. Mexicans also celebrate birthdays, baptisms, and other important occasions.

Mexican Independence Day

September 16 marks Mexican Independence Day. On this day in 1810, Mexico began a war of independence against their Spanish rulers. Spain had ruled Mexico for 300 years. Full independence was finally achieved on September 27, 1821.

Benito Juárez (1806–1872)

Benito Juárez was the first indigenous Mexican to become president of Mexico. He is considered a national hero. Juárez was born to Zapoteca Indian parents in the state of Oaxaca. During his 14 years as president, Juárez sought equal rights for indigenous Mexicans.

Every year, Mexicans celebrate their independence with flags, noisemakers, and confetti. Crowds often gather on plazas to ring bells and shout, "Long live our heroes! Long live Mexico!"

Christmas and *Las Posadas*

In Mexico, Christmas celebrations begin with *Las Posadas* ("the shelters"). Each night from December 16–24, neighbors dress in costumes and take part in a play about Joseph and Mary's journey to Bethlehem before the birth of Jesus. After the play, families gather at one neighborhood home to pray, celebrate, and break a *piñata*.

Mexican children do not receive presents on Christmas Day. Instead, gift-giving takes place on January 6. Mexicans celebrate the arrival of the Three Wise Men at the birthplace of Jesus on this day.

During *Las Posadas*, neighbors pretend to look for a house where Mary and Joseph can stay. The original story comes from the Bible.

Day of the Dead

Mexicans celebrate the Day of the Dead on the first two days of November each year. Although it may sound scary, this celebration is a cheerful time of remembering friends and family members who have died. Families visit cemeteries to leave flowers, fruits, and gifts on the graves of their loved ones. Then the families eat picnics near the graves. The picnics are supposed to make the spirits of the dead feel welcome.

Smiling skeleton dolls, candies, and masks are used to decorate homes during the Day of the Dead. The skeletons remind people of the beliefs of their **ancestors**. Indigenous Mexicans believed that the spirits of people continue to exist even after death. They believed the spirits rest until they can return to visit once a year. Today, families create altars, called *ofrendas*, with gifts, food, and burning candles to attract the spirits of their relatives during the Day of the Dead. Mexicans want the spirits of the dead to enjoy visiting the family home.

Octavio Paz (1914–1998)

Born in Mexico City, Octavio Paz is one of Mexico's most famous writers. Paz wrote many thoughtful poems and essays about Mexican history, government, and culture. He was one of the first people to write a novel with an indigenous Mexican message. In his most famous collection of essays, Paz discussed the Mexican celebration of death and the meaning of fiestas. Paz won the Nobel Prize for Literature in 1990.

Mexicans often wear skeleton costumes or masks and take part in parades during the Day of the Dead.

Infant baptism

Most Mexicans baptize their babies soon after birth. Families follow this Christian tradition of having a priest sprinkle holy water on an infant so the child will go to heaven if he or she dies. Infant baptism is also practiced by indigenous Mexicans who do not follow the Roman Catholic religion. This ancient practice is supposed to clean and protect the child from evil.

Infant baptism is an important tradition in Mexico. Family and friends gather after the baptism to celebrate with a party.

Birthdays

In Mexico, birthdays are celebrated with food, music, and games. Family and friends meet at home or a park for a party. Often, a *piñata* filled with candy is hung in a tree for the children to enjoy.

The 15th birthday is special in the life of a Mexican girl. On this day, the girl becomes a young woman. The celebration, called a *quinceañera*, is marked by a special Catholic church ceremony and then a big party with plenty of dancing. After turning 15, the young woman often gains more freedoms, such as a later bedtime.

YOUNG PEOPLE

Mexican children raised in the Roman Catholic religion take their First Holy Communion around age seven. Before the first communion, boys and girls take classes to teach them important prayers.

The children then take part in a church ceremony where they receive a piece of bread and a sip of wine to remember Jesus Christ's last supper and death. Afterward, the family usually celebrates with a party at home.

Mexican weddings

In Mexico, weddings are joyful celebrations. During a Roman Catholic wedding ceremony, the groom gives the bride 13 gold coins as a promise to take care of her. The priest or a family member places **rosary** beads or a cord in a loop around the new couple's shoulders. The loop is a symbol of the couple's love, which will hold them together in marriage. Most Mexican weddings have mariachi bands play at the end of the ceremony when the couple walks out of the church.

Wedding guests attend a lively reception following the ceremony. The guests join hands to form a heart around the bride and groom during their first dance. Music, dancing, and feasting continue for hours. The couple usually provides a *piñata* for the children.

Traditional foods at the wedding reception include soup, rice with vegetables, and meat such as pork, beef or turkey with tasty sauce. Mexicans usually eat **tortillas** with their meal. The dessert is often special wedding cookies or cake.

Did you know?

At Mexican weddings, guests usually throw red beads or rice up in the air as the newly married couple leaves the church. Loud shouting or gunfire may also follow. Friends and family want to scare away any evil spirits and bring the couple good luck.

Funeral traditions

In many cultures, a funeral would not be considered a celebration. In Mexico, funerals are an important part of life. Family and friends gather at a home to say their final goodbye to the dead person. People eat, listen to music, dance, and use the time to strengthen relationships. During the church service and burial ceremony that follows, the priest honors the dead person with words and prayers.

At funerals, family and friends are usually not afraid or embarrassed to show their feelings.

ENJOYING LIFE

Since most Mexicans work very hard, enjoying life during free time is a top priority. Mexicans like getting together at events such as sports competitions and rodeo. Many adults play sports in their own time. Tasty meals with family and friends are considered one of life's greatest pleasures.

Inside the stadium

Most Mexican towns and cities have rodeo stadiums. Mexicans gather to watch riders perform tricks and race around barrels on horseback. Some of the riders rope young cows or try to stay on top of a bucking bull.

Did you know?

In Mexico, baseball is almost as popular as soccer. Teams in the Mexican Baseball League compete every summer. Mexico has a strong national baseball team that competes against other countries.

Bullfighting is a popular **spectator sport** among Mexicans and visitors to Mexico. In bullfighting, a trained matador waves a bright red cape to make the bull angry. The **matador** then tries to kill the bull in an honorable way. When he does so, the crowd shouts "Ole!". Many people admire bullfighters for their bravery and skill. Others consider bullfighting a cruel sport in which the bull suffers stress and a painful death.

Mexicans gather in large stadiums to watch team sports. Soccer is the most popular sport in Mexico. Teams compete in a professional soccer league. When the national team competes in the World Cup competition every four years, most Mexicans watch the games on television or listen on the radio.

Rodeo riders from all over Mexico travel to compete in small towns and big cities.

Time to relax

After work is done, most Mexicans choose to relax rather than get busy with personal tasks. Mexicans often put off until tomorrow the things that are not necessary to finish today. This does not mean that Mexicans are lazy. Rather, many hard-working Mexicans value the joy of being unhurried and living in the moment.

Mexicans believe there is always enough time to enjoy a good meal with family and friends. Eating together is a way to create stronger relationships. Mexicans slow down to appreciate the food and the people. In fact, arriving on time to a dinner party is considered rude. Mexicans usually arrive at events at least 30 minutes after the proper start time.

A traditional main course at weddings is chicken or beef seasoned with cilantro and lime. Guests wrap the meat in warm tortillas. Beans and seasoned rice are common side dishes.

Some Mexicans choose to relax by watching television or going to the movies. On most Sundays movie theaters are full. Many Mexicans play soccer or baseball. Mexicans also use their spare time to read, practice dancing, or make crafts. Most of all, Mexicans use their free time to take part in activities they enjoy.

Did you know?

Corn is the most important food in Mexico. Corn provides good nutrition and is used daily in Mexican foods such as tortillas, tamales, and tacos. Mexicans add avocado or **guacamole** to many meals. Food is often seasoned with chili peppers and salsa.

Mexicans often celebrate special occasions by breaking a *piñata* filled with candy.

MEXICAN CULTURE IN THE 21ST CENTURY

Through strong relationships and religious beliefs, Mexicans have developed the ability to work hard and enjoy life to the fullest. Mexicans rely on love, loyalty, and positive thinking to face the challenges of daily life. Music, dance, art, and celebrations help them express their thoughts and feelings in meaningful ways.

Mexicans work hard to maintain traditions and beliefs in performances like this one.

Over time, Mexican culture has spread to other countries. Many people of Mexican heritage live in the United States and follow Mexican customs. *Cinco de Mayo*, a holiday celebrated on May 5 in the Mexican state of Puebla, is even more popular in the United States than in Mexico. This holiday remembers the victory of the Mexican army over the French army on May 5, 1862.

With international television, movies, and the Internet available, Mexican culture has become more similar to other large countries. Teenagers in Mexico dress a lot like teenagers in Germany, China, and the United States. However, most Mexicans continue to gather with family and friends to build relationships, pass along traditions, and celebrate important religious, historic, and personal events.

Mexicans are proud of their heritage and country.

TIMELINE

BCE

1500   The Olmecs create the first major civilization in Mexico

1200   Indigenous Mexicans begin the art of bark painting

900   Weaving is first used in Mexico to create clothing and blankets

200   The Maya paint murals to show people enjoying life

CE

1325   The Aztecs, or *Mexica*, form their civilization

1519   Spanish explorers arrive in Mexico and conquer the native people

1526   The first bullfight in Mexico takes place to honor a Spanish explorer

1531   According to legend, Our Lady of Guadalupe appears to an Aztec Indian named Juan Diego

1500s   Painted ceramic tiles are first used to decorate buildings and floors

1587   *Las Posadas* begins as a way for Catholic leaders to explain the birth of Jesus to Native Mexicans

1821   Mexicans win their independence from Spain

1861   Benito Juarez becomes the first indigenous Mexican president

1907   Artist Frida Kahlo is born

1925   The Mexican Baseball League is formed

1950   Mexican singer Juan Gabriel is born

1952   Ballet folklórico is created as a form of dance

1990   Mexican writer Octavio Paz wins the Nobel Prize for Literature

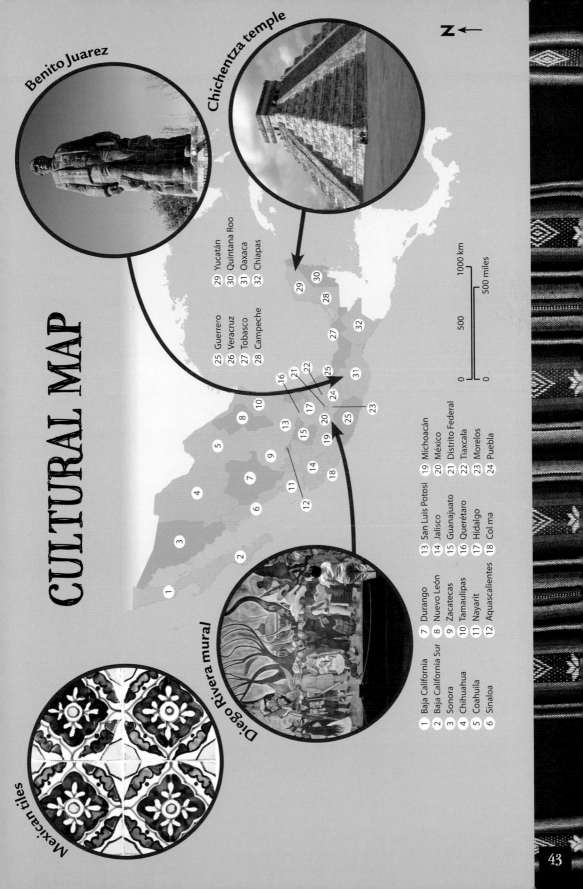

CULTURAL MAP

Benito Juarez

Chichentza temple

Diego Rivera mural

Mexican tiles

N ←

1 Baja California	7 Durango	13 San Luis Potosi	19 Michoacán
2 Baja California Sur	8 Nuevo León	14 Jalisco	20 México
3 Sonora	9 Zacatecas	15 Guanajuato	21 Distrito Federal
4 Chihuahua	10 Tamaulipas	16 Querétaro	22 Tlaxcala
5 Coahuila	11 Nayarit	17 Hidalgo	23 Morelos
6 Sinaloa	12 Aquascalientes	18 Colma	24 Puebla

25 Guerrero	29 Yucatán
26 Veracruz	30 Quintana Roo
27 Tobasco	31 Oaxaca
28 Campeche	32 Chiapas

0   500   1000 km

0   500 miles

GLOSSARY

altar raised area where religious ceremonies are performed

ancestor family relation from a very long time ago, such as a great, great grandparent

baptism religious ceremony in which a person is sprinkled or dunked in water

civilization human society that has developed an organized culture, government, and laws

colonist someone who settles in a new country, which is controlled by their government

culture customs, social organisation, and achievements of a particular nation, people, or group

custom way things have been done for a long time

embroidery art of creating raised designs with thread

fiesta Spanish word meaning party or festival

generation individuals born and living at the same time

guacamole dip made from mashed avocados, tomatoes, onions, and seasonings

heritage anything from the past handed down by tradition

indigenous original inhabitants of a certain region

matador main bullfighter whose job is to kill the bull

mural large picture painted on or attached to a wall or ceiling

native coming from a certain place or region

nuclear family father, mother, and children

piñata decorated paper figure filled with candy or toys and hung from above so that children may break it open

plaza public square or open space in a city or town

Roman Catholic branch of the Christian Church established in the second century CE. It is led by the Pope in Rome, Italy.

rosary string of beads used for counting a series of Roman Catholic prayers

rural relating to life in the country

spectator sport sport that can be watched by people who are not playing

tattoo permanent design or pattern made on the skin by inserting ink

tortilla flatbread made from corn or wheat

tradition customs that are passed on from one generation to the next

tunic loose upper body clothing that reaches to the hips or knees

weave cross threads, yarns, or strips together to make a fabric or an object such as a basket

FIND OUT MORE

Books

Brownlie Bojang, Ali. *Mexico (Countries Around the World)*.
  Chicago: Raintree, 2011.

Gruber, Beth. *Mexico*. Washington, D.C.: National Geographic,
  2007.

Johnston, Lissa. *Frida Kahlo: Painter of Strength*. Mankato, MN:
  Capstone Press, 2007.

Kalman, Bobbie. *Mexico: the Culture*. New York: Crabtree
  Publishing Company, 2009.

Websites

kids.nationalgeographic.com/kids/places/find/mexico/
Watch videos, view photographs, and read interesting
information about Mexico's land, people, and culture.

library.thinkquest.org/04oct/00633/
Find out how to make a *piñata* on this website, which is
made by and for children.

www.timeforkids.com/destination/mexico
Go virtual sightseeing in Mexican cities and learn a few Spanish
phrases on this website.

DVDs

Discovery Atlas: Mexico Revealed. Discovery Channel, 2008.
Families of Mexico. Master Communications, Inc., 2006.

Places to visit

If you ever get the chance to go to Mexico, these are some places you could visit:

Basilica de Guadalupe, Mexico City

This Catholic church stands where Mexicans believe Our Lady of Guadalupe appeared to Juan Diego in 1531. The basilica is considered by many Catholics to be the most holy place in North or South America.

Estadio Azteca, Mexico City

Watch a soccer match at the biggest soccer stadium in the world. The stadium was built in 1966 for the 1968 Olympic Games.

Lagos de Moreno, Jalisco

Experience a true Mexican rodeo at the arena in Lagos de Moreno. Mexican cowboys compete in teams in events where they show their skill on horseback.

Yucatan Peninsula

The Yucatan Peninsula is famous for its beautiful white sand beaches, sunny weather, and well-preserved Mayan ruins.

More topics to research

What topic did you like reading about most in this book? Did you find out anything that you thought was particularly interesting? Choose a topic that you liked, such as food, buildings, or religion, and try to find out more about it. You could visit one of the places mentioned above, have a look at one of the websites, or visit your local library to do some research. You could also try some things out for yourself, such as listening to *ranchera* music or watching a ballet folklórico performance!

INDEX